LIGHTNING BOLT BOOKS™

From Marbles to Video Games
How Toys Have Changed

Jennifer Boothroyd

Lerner Publications Company
Minneapolis

For my dad, who was always a kid at heart

Lerner Publications Company
A division of Lerner Publishing Group, Inc.
241 First Avenue North
Minneapolis, MN 55401 U.S.A.

Website address: www.lernerbooks.com

Library of Congress Cataloging-in-Publication Data

Boothroyd, Jennifer, 1972–
    From marbles to video games : how toys have changed / by Jennifer Boothroyd.
       p.   cm. — (Lightning bolt books™—Comparing past and present)
    Includes index.
    ISBN 978-0-7613-6746-8 (lib. bdg. : alk. paper)
    1. Toys—United States—History—Juvenile literature. 2. Games—United States—History—Juvenile literature. I. Title.
    GV1218.5.B66 2012
    790.133—dc22   2011001116

Manufactured in the United States of America
1 — CG — 7/15/11

Contents

Made for Fun

Toys and games help children have fun.

Toys and games also help children learn important skills. Both toys and games have changed over time.

Children learn how to share and take turns while playing games.

In the past, kids played with toys made from metal. They played with tin soldiers. They played with jacks.

These days, kids play with action figures.

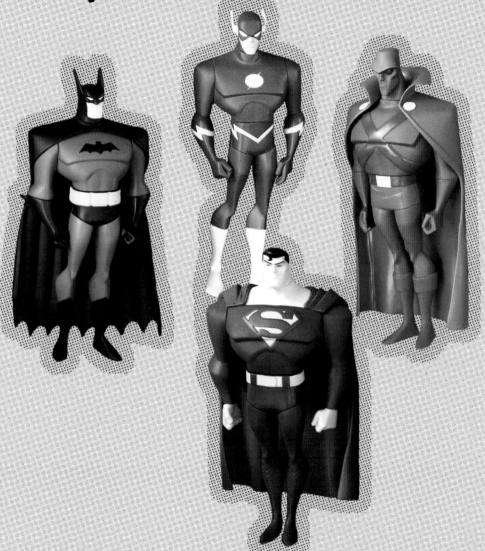

These plastic toys look like heroes from movies and TV shows.

In the past, some kids played with fancy dolls.

Some dolls were made from porcelain. Porcelain is a smooth material that breaks easily.

These days, kids play with different kinds of dolls. Some dolls talk or make noises. Some dolls have many sets of clothes.

Many dolls are made from plastic.

In the past, many toys were made from cloth or wood. Children played with fuzzy teddy bears. They played with building sets and yo-yos.

Lincoln Logs sets let kids build wooden forts and cabins.

These days, kids still play with toys made from cloth or wood.

Outdoor Fun

Many toys and games are made for outdoor play. In the past, roller skates were very popular.

Children used a skate key to tighten their skates onto their shoes.

These days,
many children
use in-line
skates or
skateboards to
roll around.

Many towns have
skate parks. These
are safe places for
children to practice.

In the past, children would play games such as kick the can or red rover.

In games of red rover, kids hold hands to form a chain. Another kid tries to run through the chain.

These days, some children still play red rover. Games such as tag and hide-and-seek are also popular.

In games of hide-and-seek, kids find a place to hide. Then another player looks for them.

In the past, hula hoops and jump ropes were very popular.

These days, many children try out these toys during gym class.

Playing with a hula hoop is good exercise.

Group Games

Many games are made to play in small groups. In the past, many children played games with marbles.

Children collected and traded marbles. In some games, children could win marbles from one another.

These days, children play games with special cards or other pieces.

Children still like to collect and trade toys and cards.

In the past, children and families played board games.

These days, people still play board games. Some games from the past use new technology.

This game comes with special electronic parts.

Video Games

In the past, video games looked very simple.

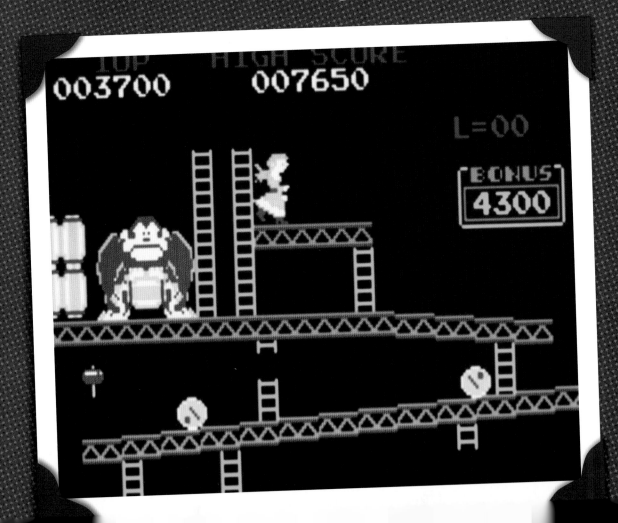

These days, video games look more colorful and exciting.

Video games changed as technology improved.

23

In the past, many people played video games at video arcades.

These days, kids play video games at home. They use a computer or hook up games to a TV.

People all around the world play video games together on the Internet.

In the past, people played video games with joysticks. Some joysticks had only one button.

Later, people used controllers with many buttons.

These days, people can play video games without using a controller.

Over time, toys and games have changed a lot. But playing with them is still an important part of a child's life.

A special camera connected to this video game captures the player's movements.

Names to Know

These people helped create toys and games for children of all ages.

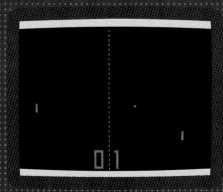

Nolan Bushnell: Nolan Bushnell created *Pong* in 1972. *Pong* is a video game version of table tennis. The game was a huge success.

Pedro Flores: Pedro Flores grew up in the Philippines. Children in this country play with a toy called a *bandalore*. The toy's wooden spool travels up and down a string. Pedro moved to the United States. He decided to sell these toys. He called his bandalores yo-yos. Pedro began the Yo-Yo Manufacturing Company in 1928.

Ruth Handler: Ruth Handler and her husband started a company called Mattel. Their daughter enjoyed playing with paper dolls. Ruth thought girls should have a plastic doll to dress up in different clothes. She introduced the Barbie doll in 1959. It was named after Ruth's daughter Barbara.

George, Charles, and Edward Parker: George Parker started a board game company in 1883. His brothers joined his company. They named the business Parker Brothers. Parker Brothers makes games such as *Monopoly*, *Clue*, and *Sorry*.

George Parker

Glossary

hula hoop: a large ring that you spin around your waist

jack: a six-pointed metal object that kids grab and toss

metal: a type of hard material such as iron, tin, or copper

plastic: a human-made material that can be molded and shaped

technology: tools, machines, and methods that people use to improve life

video arcade: a place where people pay to play video games

wood: the hard material from a tree trunk or branches

Further Reading

Heinz, Brian. *Nathan of Yesteryear and Michael of Today*. Minneapolis: Millbrook Press, 2007.

National Museum of Play
http://www.thestrong.org/online-collections/nmop

National Toy Hall of Fame
http://www.toyhalloffame.org

Nelson, Robin. *Toys and Games Then and Now*. Minneapolis: Lerner Publications Company, 2003.

Pohl, Kathleen. *What Happens at a Toy Factory?* Milwaukee: Weekly Reader Early Learning Library, 2006.

Index

Photo Acknowledgments

The images in this book are used with the permission of: © Elena Ray/Shutterstock Images, p. 2; © Flirt/SuperStock, p. 4; © Blend Images/SuperStock, p. 5; © H. Armstrong Roberts/Retrofile/Getty Images, p. 6; © Steve Skjold/Alamy, p. 7; © SuperStock, p. 8, 12, 20; © Tim Laman/National Geographic/Getty Images, p. 9; © Ed Clark/Time Life Pictures/ Getty Images, p. 10; © Jonathan Fickies/Bloomberg/Getty Images, p. 11; © Connor Walberg/Photonica/Getty Images, p. 13; © Arthur Leipzig 1943, p. 14; © Elena Rostunova/ Shutterstock Images, p. 15; © Pictorial Press Ltd./Alamy, p. 16; © OJO Images/SuperStock, p. 17; © Lambert/Archive Photos/Getty Images, p. 18; © Jenny Mattews/Alamy, p. 19; © Daniel Acker/Bloomberg/Getty Images, p. 21; © ArcadeImages/Alamy, p. 22; © Alex Grimm/Getty Images, p. 23; © Bettman/CORBIS, p. 24; © Tiny Watson/Alamy, p. 25; © JoeFox/Alamy, p. 26 (top); © James Clews/Alamy, p. 26 (bottom); © Oliver Berg/dpa/ CORBIS, p. 27; © Wendy White/Alamy, p. 28 (top); © Dennis Steen/Shutterstock Images, p. 28 (bottom); © Thomas D. Mcavoy/Time Life Pictures/Getty Images, p. 29; © Howard Shooter/Getty Images, p. 30; © Fotosearch/SuperStock, p. 31.

Front cover: © Granger Wootz/Blend RM/Glow Images (children playing video game); Minneapolis Star Journal Tribune, Minnesota Historical Society (vintage children playing marbles).

Main body text set in Johann Light 30/36.